Chris Palazzolo

Unhoused
Poems 1989–2012

regime
books

Unhoused: Poems 1989–2012
© 2013 Chris Palazzolo, who asserts all rights in relation to this work.

Published by Regime Books in Australia, 2013.
First Floor, 456 William Street, Perth.
www.regimebooks.com.au
www.twitter.com/regimebooks

ISBN 978-0-9874821-1-2

For Peter Jeffery and Liz Wisse

CONTENTS

In Oriri Ex	1
Celibate	2
X has an Adventure	4
On Being Introduced to the Poetry of Francis Webb	5
Image and Song	6
Australian Decades	9
Utopia	11
Caught!	13
Winter Verticals	15
Division	16
Open Unit	17
Unfurnished	18
Orderly Houses	19
Physics 881	24
A Star for the Speechless Sleepers	26
To Helen	27
The Float	28
Not Even Nothing	29
Where Is He Going?	30
Region	31
After Tears	32
Allegory of a Life Change	33
Peninsula Flats	35
White Noise	36
Orange	38
To the Cyborgs of the Freeway	40
The Big Wind	41
On a Lover's Hesitation	42
Tidying the Playroom	43
Isn't It Time He was Married?	44
Waking from a Dream	45
Lessons after School	46
Taken by the Swan	47
Avoiding a Pack	48

Shutting Shop	49
Holiday Home	50
A Life in Music	51

In Oriri Ex

The light cast on this page,
these lines, this twisted hand —
the serene fluorescence
of power tapped
in the caustic love-death
of carboniferous fossil
and flame twenty kilometres away.

A question for this moment:
did a tree germinate, grow,
age, and die for the illumination
of this poem, era before
the world plopped
into the bubble of an eye
thralled to a word?

Celibate

Embers of summer
smoulder in the night,

pale blue slats of streetlight
on my bedroom wall,

my skin glistening
with sweat. These are

solitude's textures,
mise-en-scene to

private habits repeated
each night unchecked by

another's eyes, reprovals
or examples of more

correct behaviours.
No. When I go to bed

the sheet covers only one
body. When I light up

a cigarette from the pillow
it is not a post-coital

smoko, reward
for discharged duties,

but merely testimony
to sleep's midsummer

resistance, when Plato's
spume and Aristotle's chess

lose their cool, fleshless
allure. Only the heat

can keep us celibates awake.
Lying on my bed

awake, bored.

X has an Adventure

After drinks and a chat
at the pub I am deposited
again on my doorstep,
a little beery from my
adventure, but otherwise
intact and still reasonably sober.

I need to expand
my horizons once in a while;
space is inseparable from air
and grows stale from overuse;
it has to be relieved
of human senses from
time to time.

My horizons are white walls
and cane blinds,
and within them I enact
those rituals of waking,
walking, eating,
and excreting, for which
sometimes only the prospect
of the pub ritual
offers any rationale.

On Being Introduced to the Poetry of Francis Webb

How small we seem
in the face of your Modern Terror, Mr Webb,
how calm, unmoved, numb.

By way of introduction, we are the ringing
in your ears after the thunderclap
of God's transformation into a meteorite — it comes
as no surprise to us
that it wasn't even for ourselves we encased
our mother in plastic and shot her
to that dead stone falling in space (they tell us
she came back but we have our doubts)

As for the words:
they are beautiful, awesome.
All we can do now
is shuffle about glass blocks
of cliché, or reconfigure and slot
sets of nothings-in-somethings into assigned spaces,
remind us of our silence, our blindness
and paralysis in the shadow of these heavy
industrial monographs of Modern Genius.

Image and Song

You are at the bottom
of a swirling trough of sea-water —
the lip, your encircling horizon,
unfurls black green high above you —
a creaming frame for a peaceful
puff of white cloud suspended
in a patch of blue,
or a white pupil in a calm blue eye
watching you, its lonely offering.

Emancipated child of the shore,
how did you stray this far?
What ghost was it you left
on that wind-terraced sand
long ago and faraway?
What shy glance
squinting in sunlight
drew you into the surf
in reckless adolescent display?
No long mornings
of thoughtless dreams
projected on your bedroom
ceiling, or fraying
narrative stitched
by contingent angel
from a rope
ever traced for you
the comedic sequence
that led you here
to your liberation —
the ocean's massive swell
has torn you from all contrivances.

Even as you start to swim,
as you gag on the first panic
cupful of brine, the cloud shredding

slowly across the sun, you know
you are palpable form
of your freedom and loss;
you know how cold
is the total, irrevocable absence
of those things
that left their mute mark on your body,
moulded with their hands
the very shape now displacing
insignificant volumes
of deep water.

Even as your arm arcs and plunges,
as if it could scoop the sea back;
freezing depths rising
into the wake of your rigid fingers,
you remember close calls,
before ingenuity
or scrambling terror brought
daylight to your eyes
and earth under your feet, when
the world's infinite circumference
shrunk to a face-full of dirt
and grassroots, or a rim
of crystalline seawater
billowing on an afternoon sky.

Once you dreamed not dreaming
haunting the horizon of your being,
surging, plunging atmospheres
beyond pinnacles of sea —
then you lay awake in darkness,
breathless, paralysed with terror,
the sun a fading photogene
on black — not until now,
until this very moment
did you ever feel so solid, so open,
and so utterly alone.

Swim! Your destiny is your next breath.
Even if your heart explode
in your chest, it will not expire
before your next breath, even
if the swell show you
beach receding, swim!
Freedom is stark necessity —
wind, ocean, and blue sky
and nothing but nothing to hold you up.

Australian Decades

Still. Midday. Air — scorched tire rubber,
baking bitumen, exhaust pipes. Prospect —
a gauze smudge of cloud above the roofs
of the northern suburbs: orange roofs,
lookout flats, eastpointing coigns
of far silver office, blur to blue-sea haze;
shimmering orange tile under coma-blue sky.

I've seen this somewhere before:
in the film *Walkabout*, which I connect
with the face of John Meillon.
John Meillon before the drink took him.
He plays the white-collar drunk
who takes his two kids out to the bush
and tries to shoot them. They escape
and he shoots himself.
A suburban loser's madness in the bush.
An Australian city under
a nineteen-sixties summer.
Call a ghost face from the shades
the sun doesn't mark decades.

Where I work money and things change hands.
Perennial transience of hands.
Even when I'm not there I see them,
the not-watching watchful salesmen
under the office eaves — pulling cuffs,
fingering white collars, puffing Winnie Reds,
scanning through sunglasses.
I see the yards reflected in their sunglasses.

Where I live the nineteen-sixties houses
on their Menzian blocks
disintegrate in the night. The Federation
miniatures which pop-up in their places
like red poppies on graves

simulate a centenary anxiety
(nostalgic cathexis of millenarian terror)
dissimulate shelters for a feral workforce,
absent by shuttered day,
shadows and noises behind
the cathode-blue security screens of night.

Utopia
Woodrow Avenue and Grand Promenade, Dianella

The streetlights do not cast pools of light
in world darkness this side of the city,
they are as close together and ambient
as the population here is said to be dense,
throwing a caul of chill visibility
on this unremarked corner —
its new traffic island and cracked footpath,
derelict's-hair grass and cigarette-butt dirt
in kerb gaps, its bus-stop, Keep Left
and No Parking At Any Time signs —
nocturnal fluorescent daylight
for the populations
haunting their well-lit spaces
with their well-policed absences
while anomic freeways faraway breathe
across the wide open channel of air.

The houses wear rust and sandstone masks
but notwithstanding paranoia's
curtain-crack eye and button-numbering thumb
are blind. Huddled in the exotic shadows
of their front yards — rootless palms
and chainsaw-disciplined gums —
paths draped across mist blue lawns
like sleeping tongues
tasting the open footpath —
or hidden by two metre sandstone
verge walls bearing the elbow tags
of the hooded ones with spraycans —
they are the silent carnival
of the population's shells, and inside each one,
cocooned in their beds,
populations dream of never having walls.

A car approaches down the fluorescent canal
of the Avenue. Suddenly, imperceptibly,

time recurs — noise and displaced air
of the hurtling object slowly detach
from the surrounding matrix of sonic surf —
a red Toyota Seca, cones of headlights
bisect the molecular streetlight,
fleeting geometries of torn light flit and slip
across its red skin and black windscreens,
turbulence now warping through the world.
As it nears the corner and slows,
its dashboard-lit driver
can just be discerned — a staring organism
in a greenish-blue solution.
      It passes...

  If someone is awoken in the houses
there is no sign — no muted light of a bedlamp,
no sleepy eye through a blind. Maybe
it is being dreamed of too,
this solitary midnight car, in its passing,
as it turns right onto Grand Promenade,
its deep-throat exhaust pipe blowing,
and accelerates away? Maybe
it is being dreamed of as lost, winding its way
through the night suburbs before it finds itself
on those faraway freeways
where it will circulate forever?

Caught!

Again freezing wind-fist punches me
flings nicks of rain onto the footpath and crashes
through the verge tree over me —
tortured leaves thrash —
demented branches slash — over me bough groans.

Rain-dot spats the corner of my mouth
moistens the seal of my lips
foretaste of what's waiting four strides further —
I'm going to get wet — my house
is on the other side of the road I'm 45-degree
blunt-knifing through keen rain-spiked wind towards
and I'm going to get wet.

First contact my right temple inclined forth
to shear the front —
cheeks, bridge of nose and shoulders
to split it wide to drag the mass of my body through —
my legs forward propelling off concrete
that my lips would kiss,
my nose bloody were it not
for cheek-blustering will-pummelling squalls —
my faceflesh is stiffening
icy needles will collide with pinkening porcelain.

I don't have to look up to see the sky is iron cold
and lowering on my head
my eyes just have to fix on the footpath before me
and they will see it spread
into a sagging belly of swollen stormsky slit open
spilling grey curtains of mist
already veiling the forms of trees houses and road
that used to be my world
until my wind-ploughing body and tormented tree
are all that remain, relieved against

this air-stuffed second before water thrashing —
a spit of lightning and a golden bough and I'll be a myth —

    Stamp, in the mind-matter of frozen time,
              a running man and tree —
    slash, for the field of wind and water,
              horizontal lines —
    and string from sky to bough
             a thread of holiest gold—

But if I'm spared transfiguration
by the time I reach my doorstep
my jumper's sodden hem will be slung below my knees

Winter Verticals

*Winter-world, wrap me
in your restless atmospheres
tug at my coat and jeans
brush me across
the street before it rains again*

The bus drives off in spray —
a rugged-up man
walking briskly across the street corner —
a homing man and wintry houses —
wind-tossed sun-green gumtrees,
a swooning palm —
a gaunt berg
of thundercloud
to the
apogee
of the sky

The cloud
is passing across
remote mid-afternoon sun —
dizzying verticals
of light
off fleeting mountaintop
The darkening
street corner
is deserted,
the man
rushed
home

Division

Why get out of bed if I'm still asleep? The warm
sweet ribbon of tea slips down some gullet
only remotely mine. Somewhere else
I'm still dreaming. But I'm so sick of dreams.

I have swapped flats with my friend for a change
of scene — (a white door, a hand turning a ceramic
doorknob, absent room) — eyes open. I'm still in bed.
Rise again. Drift through a flat in a work-world
already three hours old.

The other night my friend spoke about ghosts.
A ghost is a physiology buried
under a physiology. Freud located them
in the language. He called them
ellipses and lacunae, and traced their movements
through the workplaces and classrooms
into the playgrounds and bedrooms of the mind.

Do I take my buried physiology
still naked under the blankets with me
clothed to the kitchen? Does it get as far
as the shops to buy the paper, bread, and margarine?

What does it want to do? To write, to read,
to eat, to fuck, or watch tv? If this physiology is the one
with the teeth, what does it want to bite?

Open Unit

Our unit is up for sale; us humble renters
in a buyer's market; from up there
what we call home must look
like Opportunity.

Phone call in the morning:
The Professionals Realty, agent's name
and a possible investor
(fingers crossed). They come from elsewhere
these investors, the ruling sphere
of buying and selling, and here they are —
a sport-label couple, a grey suited woman,
the agent with a card in our loungeroom.

I've opened all the windows
so it's nice and airy,
made the bed, chucked the clothes
in the wardrobe; play the responsible tenant
in a nice and airy investment. And they
walk through — investor-vision eyes
piercing our transparent furniture
to the skirting we will only see again
when we move.

One of our arrangements
must be pretty opaque though — our bed
in the dining area (for the bedroom is pokey
and the kitchen window lets in
the coolest breeze). Nonetheless
we are weightless things. A gust of summer
wind will blow us both out one day.

Unfurnished

A notice to vacate this unit finally sent,
but the membrane of home has already split and starting to peel.
I feel the tender etiolated corners
to be exposed when we start to pack. I sense that time
has taken here, eating away at this terminal space
like rust in guttering. Soon we will be vagrants
in vacant rooms, echoes off alien walls.

To look at us right now you would never guess
we are loosening like poorly glued bathroom tiles
or lifting like cheap parquetry. The imminent dismantling
of our domestic organon has only begun
to shadow our minds. Our routines continue throughout the day
and following days, but we are already ghosts
already translucent. In my mind the shadow will assume
its formless form, for I now see the chaos of boxes;
random cuboid objects tumbling in disoccupied space.

Orderly Houses

1. House

Humans never meet the Men that built
their houses, for the hands that poured
the cement, lay the bricks, fitted the sills,
lay the tiles, nailed the beams, wired, plastered,
and skirted the walls, might have perished
æons ago, so anonymous and so mute are the marks
they leave behind: a brick upon a brick, a broken
brick for plumbing, a brick in a wall, in a wall
a window, screwed to the wall
a rainpipe attached to guttering, out there
shrinking and expanding with the storms
and still of the infinitely open; crust of canyons,
canals of grey cement, troweled plateaux,
then wind; the inner face of the wall
smothered over with plaster then a film
of paint or wallpaper, to absorb the
accretions of human economy.
If it can be supposed that each brick records
the planetary inscriptions of materiality
and love, objects and affects, what stories
of housebound humans would a house play back?
If footsteps down a hall, or arguments muffled
by a bedroom door, the daily routines
of working, eating, procreating, excreting,
leave acoustic copies, vibrations veined
through the substance of the walls fleshed
by the iterability of ritual and the exquisite
counterpoint of contingency, what poem
of animate and inanimate would it sing?

2. Houses

(Report from the periphery) — At night,
particularly clear, still nights under a full moon,

the older houses around here have faces that watch,
profile or portrait. Blind faces, frozen in laughter
or discourse: a dark veranda
an open crocodile mouth; a red path
leading from the veranda to the front gate a thin,
red lolling tongue; two tall rectangular windows eyes
upturned to the starless sky. A kind of cubist face:
the upturned eyes next to the open mouth,
not above it, and both on the same side. The nose,
it seems, is missing (or perhaps that shadowy
extension next to the eyes? Or the letterbox
on the tip of the tongue?). Another may have one
wide loungeroom-window eye
staring out from a behind a fence like a child
with a hand across its face (lying or shy?).
Next door to the child, one with two small square
windows, too small and close together
like hayseed eyes, set in a blank beige wall. And yet
another frowning under its gables, the powerline
plugged into its forehead a thread of distress
from a fossil burning in a distant metal chamber.
Suburban pictographs legible
only to the solitary noctambulator
who will assume late at night
when most houselights are out,
that there are humans inside, sleeping,
viewing films gooey with love's ectoplasm.

3. Home

Human, you don't finish at the skin. The skin
of my forearm in a room, crater mouths
of pores exhale oily plumes of perspiration,
lunar puffs of dead skin-cell fragments,
cataclysmic impact of partial bodies,
whipped up by micro-eddies, trail thinning spinning debris
above the follicle savannah puff slow-motion
into atmosphere. Human, space for you
is something made not something given.

But that wall is no design of mine, I didn't
put it there. Human, it teeths its being
on your disavowing. Open or closed
you will be the medium of its sound.
Bring in objects, furniture, books, clothes, food,
things have roots push down into
your orphan being, earthed still to the mother
of clay, baked and veined. But you move
across it. Leave a ghost behind. Radiate
everyday actions. Can you see, in a time-lapse
film. Watch the white lines you leave. White blotches
burn into the film. Who are you?
Human, questioning you make me a questioner.
The portrait is good, the question-sound
hollow echo in eternity. There is no one else
here, you ask yourself a question.
Are you a relation of mine? I am relations.
Only you can close the circle
of our acoustic affinity, then I visit, then your skin,
which knows better, will puck

4. Men

Where it sits right now, this night wanderer,
this skin-sealed human by day, whose desire
was it to have its house built here? From what distant
constellation of legislative and speculative data
did the command issue forth those many æons ago
for a dwelling to be fabricated
on this prehistoric dirt? A new alignment configures
in the digital firmament out of which a giant Pointing Hand
emerges with a clap of thunder: bring Men
from those Lands, bring Materials from those Lands,
unite them in this Land right here
under the Ægis of Capital, between the pegged string
marking the parameter of the dirt surveyed,
upon the steel grating pinning the sheets
of black plastic flapping in the breeze, the bags
of cement, the cement mixer, the spade-bitten pile

of yellow sand, the aluminium-strapped blocks
of bricks — water, wood, copper, brick, glass, steel,
concrete, aluminium, plastic — and Men, eyes behind
their wrap-around sunglasses, eardrums thrumming
to FM radio. They are humans too,
related to materials and their forms by far more
than Money's Hymeneal. They have houses. They
view films inside.

5. Bricks (Ode to a Demolished House)

In the end, a big dusty pile of broken bricks
many still stuck with the grey strip of cement
which joined them to other bricks
when they were one and home.
How many broken recordings of lives continue
their feeble tremors in this rubble,
after the shock of demolition, when the iron teeth
of the grader's shovel bashed
into a middle row and brought the rest crashing
down in ground-shaking whumps of dust
and fragments? There they lie, once proud
suburban walls, once sharp coigns that cleaved
the tempestuous winds, once ordered rows
that bore the weight of the roof and suffered
the cricket balls and removalists of outrageous
fortune. No more lives for them to record
or ghosts of blunted purposes to play back.
This little world is finished, smashed down,
its wooden skeleton flayed
and exposed, emptied, the aftermath of a war
in a subdivision. The windows crashed open
and whatever screams and laughter
of recorded souls that dwelled there have fled.
Let these brief lines be its last song,
before the ruins are dumped onto a truck
and taken to be pulverised, and the subcontrators
of forgetting arrive to start building next week.

6. Orderly Houses

Orderly houses. Endless rows of houses.
Hundreds of thousands, millions of houses,
houses to the sea-sky blue. Still, silent faces
on the outside, sticky and webby on the inside,
every one, with human love, hate, sorrow, boredom,
dreams, and routine thoughtlessness, on top of all
the past lives, ghosts of relatives orthodox,
eccentric, and exiled that persist upon
their living hosts in the carpeted passages and rooms.
Trillions of brick cassettes recording all that comes
and goes, all that's said, suffered, celebrated, silent,
all that lives and dies. Orderly rows of bricks
with very high quality recordings,
exquisite counterpoint of vibrations
defying stasis in their slow erosion over decades,
soundless countless oscillations
harmonising with acoustic fields of human presence,
engendering spectres which haunt every film
and waking transaction. And the humans
whose hands lay the bricks, fitted the sills, et cetera?
We will not speak of them for they perished æons ago
and their bodies have become dust.
As Men they Rose from the Dead it's True,
they are making Money like me and you.

Physics 881

The edge of the station concourse sweeps overhead.
The curtain of late morning light lifts on a 20 minute bus-framed
   commuter culture,
      this one of uni students: backs of tousled heads;
one male reading profile in the seat
  near the front; a girl with clean torn jeans
      in the seat across from me, three seats
         from the back, gazing out the window.
We share the same destination, occupy the same cuboid space in time
   but only the two girls on the back seat are nattering.
     Concrete walls stream past the windows, drop away,
          and reveal to my unsurprisable commuter eye
       the state's financial glacier colonising the sky,
             moving slowly to the past.
    A nerve twinges in my skull; I put on sunglasses.

In an insulated space we hurtle through space to fold up
              time in a timetable.
The freeway can never be satisfying,
  it can never be as smooth as not being at all.
    There is always time to pass, places to cross,
       and a world to hew into shape.
The buzz of the tire treads pounding the bitumen
  every hundredth of a second vibrates in my bones.
      My guts know we are moving.
        My head? It knows too, calmly detached
      in a paradigm of schedules.
  It knows something has to happen between there and there:
    I skim the readings for today's tutes.
            I stare out the window and daydream.

Despite post-modernity the seasons are doing their midyear turnover —
  purple ranges of stormcloud heaped on the horizon —
    you see such things from a bus window along the riverside stretch
      of freeway —

tucked in this rattling pocket of velocity —
you see the world as a multiplicity of bodies and speeds
and the body at rest as fastest of all.

A Star for the Speechless Sleepers

First star on a silver field.
Across the eyeline of the fence,
perigee for an absent eye,
black scarab of lamppost, and a distant gum on ice-red ribbons of cloud,
an infinity of whitening sky with a tincture of scarlet.
A tv aerial draws spectral fluid
from this mute and breathless field,
but we don't reconstitute those bodies and their chattering heads —
this evening, sleep is our substitute for speech.

Lullaby —

    The window is open, the world outside recedes,
    the swell of blanket and quilt slowly deepening.
    You have let go of everything beyond the borders of your bed,
    only your sleepening heavy bodies smoothly sinking.

    Both of you can go into your separate cells now:
    security lights tick-rigid-flick-on in the antechamber.
    As you pass into penumbra of storms of the other side,
    ghostly clunking of the system's plumbing grows louder.

To Helen

Think back to the day we first meet —
on the Safety Bay beachfront beneath the pines;
me, an incongruous wraith in tobacco-fumed black
and black mushroom-mop hair; you,
a watchful beachside stroller,
sandals in hand, quite in your element
in your denim shorts and blue tank-top
floppy straw hat with blue ribbon and bow.
Blue seabird meets black alleycat by the beach.
The seabird can fly away if she wants. She doesn't.

It is early Spring. A seabreeze pushes
silly cottonbuds overhead, quick shadows
run the grass where we meet and talk.
We will be a couple:
we will go down to the shore and stroll
meandering terraces of seaweed along the sand.

The Float

When we were together
we were like pegged currencies
and sex was our Gold Standard —
it never lost its lustre
but restricted the range of our emotions
within a narrow band
of fluctuations that soon chafed
and diminished their value
causing inflation in depression
and falling profits in love

Not Even Nothing

I dreamt you!
I dreamt you collapsing
melting as in your poem —
the flesh bones and organs
liquefying in acid tears
and pooling around my feet —
I awoke to plups of vitreous
jelly and blood squirting
the last of you

You're all over me
this poem you sprayed over me
like a squid spurting ink —
I'm covered with it
stained disgraced and abominable

What vengeance!
I can't even say I'm nothing
for look what I did to you
and even worse look
what you are now
The Poet
and me not even nothing!

Where Is He Going?

Late-night cars whisper to me
mysterious errands and clandestine rendezvous.
My door is open on the cool gloom
and out there in the probing headlights I roam.
There I am, near the bus-stop
long after the busses have run
or walking the footpath by the cyclone fence
that borders the invisible reserve.
We are companions in mystery
me and these passing cars.
What thoughts gnaw in those dark cabins
I'll never know,
and where does that solitary man walk
at this late hour? Where?

Region

I claim more time with
each word and a space clears
around me: the live ends
of my world can touch again—
the radio playing quietly
in the loungeroom behind me —
the door before me open
on the cool gloom —
the musk of displaced dust
after a spattering of rain —
a bin lid clattering in the lane —
all these things will continue
in their own way
when these words cease,
and so I guess will I, though
something will remain here,
I don't know what,
and I don't know how they relate.

After Tears

After tears I am clean and empty
I have no feelings anymore.
Season turning,
cooler nights, dark by six.
I still write by an open door.

I'll write properly
of my exposure soon
when it's cold.
I will use this thin ink
to eke me out here naked
and thin
but alive yet.

Allegory of a Life Change

1

Dry grass on a far coast. The coast is near, but never before seen. We have driven past it many times. Now I'm walking down its slope, feeling the wind tufting my hair. Great jetties a long way away. The sea before me is all grass, daffodils and dandelions, bees and cicadas. Boats are skiing through it. It is all awave like the sea in a breeze. I am swimming through it, even the dirt parts and waves, tangled stems of grass and bushes that curl up above me and roll over me. There are shops and a change-room block next to the shore. My wife was there going for a stroll. She has gone home now. It is getting late. A long cloud leaning across the sky, pulling evening behind it. Terror is growing in my guts. I am alone. The world is futureless.

2

I am standing in the crater of a big rock. The rock is falling in space. Vacuum surrounds it to infinity. In that infinity are stars. The stars stay still even though there is wind. The wind is blowing, beating, pushing across the rock, blowing things off it, sand and little rocks, grass and seeds, out into space. Moonlight is on the rock. I am going to be blown off. I crouch down until my fingers can touch the cold surface of the rock. Wild wind pummels me. I lie down in the crater and curl up. I can never move again.

3

Late morning sunshine, clear sky. The rock is behind me. Somehow I got off it. Turns out to have been a building. My university. Long stone steps leading away. Finally got away. Suburbs in the hills. Taupe patch of pine plantation, sweet smoke of summer, burnoff distant haze. Willy-willies on the broad hills, black Vonnegut worms squirming upright across the crests. I am in mum's car in the hills, the university behind us. Further away, no going back. One of the willy-willies is coming towards us, across the houses and onto the streets. Trees and powerlines whip into its swarming funnel, growing bigger, towards the car. Hits us car is shook. Gone. Bright sunny day. Further away. No going back.

Peninsula Flats

Strange the rhythms of my contact
with the other tenants here. I was certain
the couple next door were going to split up
but she got pregnant instead and does her washing
in the laundry barefoot. I've seen her a lot
recently, her belly starting to distend,
and as always she smiles at me nicely
when we greet each other
from our doorsteps. I haven't seen him for weeks.

The little Maltese gentleman on the top floor
has disappeared as well. He'd spend all day
during the summer leaning on the balustrade
with his glass of red wine
and the full sun on his bald head, greeting me
and everyone passing
with a cheery familiarity which I often found
annoying, but to tell the truth I miss now.
The courtyard in the vacant flat next door
is watered every day I get home from work
so he must be still around.

Close, but with no question or desire to share —
I have my cave to potter and sleep in, my kettle
boiling for a cup of tea. The comings
and goings of others can remain safely
a mystery of only momentary interest to me,
enough, perhaps, to provide a subject
of these jottings once the door is closed, the tea
poured, and the sound of evening news
floats down from the flat above.

White Noise

Midnite tv noise — lonely hearts/
phone now/WA Salvage/CNN Americana —
celibate seen-the-light salesvoices
(here's a picture of it!) booming there,
shifting gently through the curtain here
with a sighing sough.
                softly breeze
As is the custom I will picture him:
my blue-stoned midnite neighbour
lying on his sofa watching tv.

Beyond these suburban dog-ears
of low light and noise, mine and his,
the city is a far roar,
like a jumbo jet forever taking off,
forever unfolded, forever taking off
far away, a ubiquitous white roar
unfurling under the desert's night sky —
metallic trails of truck's gears
or police sirens miles away,
beyond so many vacant bus-stops,
readerless signs on yellow posts,
deserted footpaths, distant and more
distant walls (streetlit black coignlines),
mothflecked lightpoles vanishing
rows down highways and freeways,
are the only other sounds,
sonic scrawls on its vast open whiteness.

Who of us is really awake,
him with his images, me with my text,
immersed in or scratching down signs?
Who of us will go outside
and walk these homeless spaces far away,
not in dreams, not in daydreams or words?

The hole in our hearts is an empty channel
through which we speak our love for our terror.
Who of us will speak now,
form words never spoken
out of this wordless void in white noise?

Orange

That's me: a gull that propels itself
against a driving shelf of air
above the surf,
fixed to a line
of will-to-fly-forward, mass,
and the will-less force
of onshore winds which
stick it to a point,
a little pennant on the turning earth
as the sun touches the sea.

I haven't moved from this spot
for a long time now.
My will to keep moving
can only keep me motionless
or at least on course
among a disparate jumble
of fellow tumbling things.
To get the bills and rent paid,
to keep fed and clothed,
to keep my good humour
among friends and family
is a struggle
and need, from love
and a drive that will not die.

I know the will-less one in myself
in the gull, and in the wind,
means it is all outside,
danced by forces we can't comprehend,
and yet its fingers are nuanced
by a force to make the will.
Only when its fingers
break open the seat of our identity
like our fingers break open an orange
can we find the force to intend

has been intended for us,
or at least a minor clause
in some nameless grammar.

To the Cyborgs of the Freeway

Should your Neurofen nerves be speared by a sunray,
and the Excell spreadsheet en-grid the day,
think first of the KPIs you're achieving,
and then of all the money you're receiving,
above all think that when the deal is clocked,
the car locks chirp, and the seatbelt locked,
the cyborg awakes when the petrol ignites,
glides onto the freeway's trance of headlights,
forgets the workplace it left behind
and erases the destined home from its mind,
sublating the weight of duty and need
into a stereophonic capsule of speed —
a man-machine's ecstatic perceiving
of a strip of dusty spectrum for evening.

The Big Wind

The Big Wind blows
the football results away,
and airs the houses of winter smells.
He throws the trees into wild swoons,
makes the powerlines skip
and the washinglines whip and snap.
You can hear his laughter
as he rolls across the groaning roofs;
his beard is a cumulus of billowing air,
his breath the ghost of burnt eucalyptus,
and his eyes twinkling desert stars.
With a sweep of his arm he hurls
summer's invisible breakers
on the shores of the city.

On a Lover's Hesitation

When is the right time?
When the stars are aligned
on their most auspicious axis.

Time is always wrong.
There is always something
not finished
or still missing
but will be found
has to be found
because it was once there
and cannot be nothing.

Perhaps it will come with you
this missing
when the wrong time
you make the right time
on nothing more than starlight
flings you into a new orbit
of troubles and promise?

Tidying the Playroom

The broken toys speak
puppet plays of superhero battles
and dinosaur and dinky-car classrooms —
a carpet-bombing of smaller and still
smaller partial objects: a Transformer wheel,
a Ben 10 arm, a Dalek stalk, a plastic
bubble blower, a vinyl pouch, a pile
of naked contorted Barbies, that no inventory
of coloured bins, baskets,
and biscuit tins can ever sufficiently order.

These walls mark off from the rest
of our incubator home the site
of *infans industria*. The suspension
bridges, train networks
and particle accelerators of the future
may have their origins here,
but right now it is the law
of entropy that is tested
with the concentration
of an experiment, a kind of furious shredding
of the world by a myriad
of quickly discarded childish plots.

Praise the state for school — those benevolent walls
absorbing all that kiddie productivity.

Isn't It Time He was Married?

The everopen footpath
where I dream an everother self —
I walk it night after night, naked,
yet to be seen, expecting exposure
in a hot light that never seems
to turn on me, seeing the people
who do not see, the cars
that do not stop, feeling the shame
that burns my face, the terror
that shrinks my skin. When I awake
I'm in my bed, but I can't remember
whether I came in through the door,
or streamed through the porous walls,
for I'm convinced I was out there
and it's only a matter of time before
I'm seen on the everopen footpath
living an everother self.

Waking from a Dream

Our voices are frightened, the fear crowds in
like a bell of shadow —
                      I'm awake.
My mind is clean.
I'm breathing my wife's bare shoulder, an aching
horn on her thigh. I could try, but I'll probably
get an elbow for my trouble.

So I get up and marvel at a loungeroom
of renewed dimensions: how our black sofas
triangulate me, how the bookcase,
tv cabinet, and stereo crowd the space
behind me; involvements revealed
in dormant hours; I picture
in this perfect stillness the kids jumping
from sofa to sofa, the grownups slumping
in front of tv; an intimate topography
unveiled in the alignment of lamplight
and mind lucid, open, and companionable
among these things.

Lessons after School

The lessons don't stop
once she's outside the school:
there's the crossing at the flag
and the lugging of her bag;
impress upon her vital little body
weight and apportionment.
For the rest of the journey
it's the slack and pull
of paternal gravity: he pays out,
lets the girl run ahead
and hug a classmate; he notes
her delight at this contact
after school, but does not break
his stride; with an eye
on that head of stormcloud
calculating the minutes
for the arrival of rain,
he keeps on walking,
until his departing shoulders
tug the girl away and she slouches
on behind him towards home.

Taken by the Swan

He will take one of us when he can,
our shy and secretive Swan,
he moves faster than you think.
The boy ducks; torchlight
slashes the butt of wall,
the knot of trees on the bank —
freedom is a short swim
from where he squats,
panting at how quick it all fucked up
and frantic to hear his grandma's voice —
drawn to the playful gurgle at the roots
he doesn't have time to think…

    even the constable is tempted —
that tape of moonlit silver,
so narrow you could step over it.

Avoiding a Pack

This is the worst place for an encounter:
on a long street at the dark corner
of the block; the bang
of a kicked fence up ahead, and two, three,
no, four male silhouettes on the footpath;
too late to halt, turn, and walk back,
no sidestreet to veer into,
and ducking behind a letterbox
or hedge one of those panic actions
guaranteed to transmogrify
group and individual into pack and prey.

So just walk. Don't speed up. Don't
slow down. If one sneers, 'How's it goin'?'
say, 'Good,' and ignore them
parroting your weird voice; you'll see shortly
the uprooted plants and overturned bin,
and know what they have in store
for the fool who signals 'hit me.'

Shutting Shop

The last customer hurries her choice
and exits the shutting shop: the sign
is in, the float boxed, the take signed
and bagged. As he thinks of the thousand
times he's turned this key and rattled
the door to confirm it's locked,
perhaps he'll never have to work
a final shift. If he peers through
the window one last time
perhaps he'll see himself in a thousand
tomorrows still standing at that till.

Holiday Home

The newest sunlight falls across the step
the hall swallows the key's fiddlesome noise
the kids forget their car-seat gripes
and go hunting for the toys.

The grownups stock the cupboards and drawers
and choose the beds that they will make
auditing each musty room
for items that could break.

Tasteful prints on spotless walls
connote comfort in the enigmatic
like dinky drawers and tables in corners
exposed to children's traffic.

The house will tolerate the intrusive bustle
for the contracted days they're there:
the sprawl of bags on bedroom floors
or an esky on a chair.

It will wait through the slow sightseeing hours
let its neutral décor speak
then absorb a child's sleepy night-time cry
at an unfamiliar creak.

For when the family finally pack and leave
there is no more reason to hide
the holiday home is only a home
when no one is inside.s

A Life in Music

For Chris Boyder

There / Not there.
Is this what a zygote thinks
when it hears that steady thumping?
Or is that thumping a kneading thumb
that shapes its waist, moulds
the back of its legs, the crook
of its arm, pinches around the helmet
of head and shoulders
to make a neck
while the sifting silting fibres
of cell work grow?

Of course hearing and thought
come later, perhaps around the age
of that little Viennese boy
who threw his toy
beneath the bed and cried, 'Gone!'
and then cried, 'There!'
when it was retrieved.
The doctor thought
the boy unremarkable
but should've recognised a prodigy
who discovered before language
the simplest pair of tones —
Aaaah / Ooooh —
There / Not there.

This pair grew in complexity
a sifting silting of tones
which built into notes.
The boy grew and all around him
the brushing stroking pushing
and pulling notes shaped him.
His mother sang
in the nursery,
the choirs sang in church,

men scraped notes
from pieces of wood on street corners,
as if they all knew this game
of what is and what is not —
There / Not there.

At school he sang
the Emperor's songs
and took his place as a theme
one of many in a whole
with the Sovereign as the key
for the Emperor wasn't there
he was Everywhere —
There / Not there
at the same time.

And this whole was many
and had many names,
from songs of childhood, to etudes
of adolescence, to sonatas,
concertos, and symphonies
of early manhood.
Mozart, Haydn,
Beethoven, and Schubert,
all turned upon the key
that kept the whole in place,
kept the up from the down,
the start from the finish,
the There from the Not There
for only the key could be both.

Brahms, Wagner,
Bruckner, and Mahler —
striving and will became complexity.
The whole began to slide
and warp in the delirium
of its overcoming,
until they split the key itself
and made it many.

In the silence that preceded
the applause in a hall
Not There
was loudest of all.

When the whole was threatened,
he wore the Emperor's uniform
he held the Emperor's gun,
he shot other young men
off mountainsides.
Not There, he thought
when he saw their bodies fall
Not There forevermore
and the whole
became the nothingness
that swallowed the Emperor too.

A democracy of tones swarmed
like people clamoring for food.
He had a sick wife
and children to feed,
labour blind without hope
or identity, equal in a series
of individuated atoms
building the incomprehensible
monstrous modern
without a key to stop the clash
of dialectics and might
and clandestine jazz
insinuating from another world.

Did he live to hear
these particle worlds emerge?
Or did he perish in the cacophony
of their collisions?
He has many alternate lives and deaths
precisely because we do not know.
Perhaps in one he lives
to a very old age?
Perhaps his last years are spent

in that other world
amid a syncopation of cars,
bungalows, and palms?
Perhaps he sits blanket on knees
and hears a symphony on a radio
and for a duration the key is restored
up is up, down is down,
There is There, and Not There
there as well?
Schrödinger's Cat
The Man Who Mistook His Wife for a Hat

Acknowledgements

Some of these poems have appeared in *Marginata* and *Creatrix*. 'A Life in Music' was commissioned by Chris Boyder for double-bass accompaniment. Special thanks to Nathan Hondros and Regime Books for encouraging fresh voices to dispel the terrible Westralian silence.

www.ingramcontent.com/pod-product-compliance
Lightning Source LLC
Chambersburg PA
CBHW030226170426
43194CB00007BA/874